Pandora's Box
Creative Magazine

Spring 2019

pandorasboxmag.weebly.com
fb.com/pandorasboxmag

Cover photo:
Sunset on 45th Street
Charlie Bush

Spring 2019 Staff & Contributors

Editor-in-Chief: Kristie Huang
Vice President: Julia Cheunkarndee
Head Layout Officers: Sandra Chiu, Rida Khawaja
Layout Officer: Charles Swaney
Managing Officers: Hannah Kim, Liza Kolbasov, Kristen Yee
Fundraising Officers: Carly Feng, Justin Lee
Publicity Officers: Rachel Cai, Hailey Leclerc, Rajat Khar
Club Advisor: Mr. Dunlap

2019-20 Officers-in-Training:
Aarohi Gupta, Clarissa Kam, Daniel Barczczak, Jonathan Fang, Lillian Fong, Liza Kolbasov, Melissa Ding, Rida Khawaja, Sophia Lu, Sulaiman Khawaja

Key Contributors:
Aarohi Gupta, Clarissa Kam, Daniel Barszczak, Emily Shen Jay Li, Jonathan Fang, Katherine Killion, Lillian Fong, Mishaal Hussain, Nora Dee, Shana Ebrahimnejad

Pandora's Box Creative Magazine has been a part of Henry M Gunn High School's student community for over 20 years.

We are a student-run literary & creative magazine, featurin work by student artists, poets, writers, and photographers. *Pandora's Box* provides an outlet for students to explore thei creativity and showcase their talent.

Artwork

Questions of the Soul
Erin Vetter

will I be a name to memorize,
a soul to forget,
or will I fade away into a stack of numbers registered as
deaths.
will I be remembered in terms of love,
will I be forgotten in terms of history.
will one place contain my story or
will my life not be captured at all.
will I be grouped in with others completely different; a life
misunderstood.
will my name be remembered,
or will I just be a nameless body.
will my love be saved by the one who owns my heart,
will a legacy be something that is left by me.
will I be stuck forever in a painting or a photo,
will I ever be recognized in one.
and all I am in the end is a bundle of memories contained in a
life,
asking at the dividing line if I stay in minds and hearts or if I
leave quick.

this is where it gets me;
what will be remembered of me,
and will I be forgotten completely?

Untitled
Livia Bednarz

Still, Life
Caroline Ro

Daj with Four Arms

Sofía Sierra-García

Cookie Cutter Emotion

Ruhi Mistry

What does love feel like? I know what it feels like for objects; I love lists and cheap ramen and embroidery and Broadway musicals, but in my mind, those are just the good things in the world that you attach the title of love to because you want to show how you identify with it. I know what it's like to love your parents and your friends, but that's a kind of aching in your gut that you're never really aware of until you find yourself missing them after they're gone, or when you go out of your way to do nice things for seemingly no other reason than friendship.

But love, the idea, and feeling of it is frustratingly undefinable. Attachment is easy to understand, why isn't that the "go to" feeling? No one tells their wife, "I'm attached to you." No one writes songs about wanting to be with someone because you can't imagine life without them and labels it attachment. If you asked ten people what love was, in any definition from the most scientific to the most abstract, no one would give the same answer. Love is when someone tells you to get home safe. Love is an emotional minefield. Love is when your heart rate quickens. Love is a mixture of hormones being released in your brain. Love is commitment. Everyone has their own definition, but does everyone know what it means? What it feels like? What it's supposed to feel like? Adults say I love you before they know what it means, children say I love you knowing exactly what it means.

And why do you need it? It's such a major goal for so many people, and media blares at us through everything from kids shows to Hallmark movies that it's all we should focus on. Yes, it's nice to have someone else who's always on your team, but isn't that what friends are for? Why not marry your best friend for tax benefits and live a romance-free life? Love your friends, love movies, love everyone. Don't pour all your attention into anything. Don't make someone else your world, what if they can't be there forever? I should be a whole person without someone else.

Love shouldn't make us feel isolated and agonized because of what it's made out to be. Love should be the satisfaction of eating cheap ramen, the giddiness you get after embroidering a cactus. Love should be the bittersweet feeling after you say goodbye to your friends. Love should be your mom making you a snack when she sees you've been studying for hours, your dad reading a book in your room because he wants to be near you. Love should be whatever you define it to be. And that should be enough.

Piano

Anonymous

I fidgeted; my hands were sweating,
and my heart was beating like
hummingbirds' wings. I was the next
performer. I hadn't even known that I
needed to play a solo piece until the last
rehearsal before the concert. It was only
ten seconds before my performance. I
took a deep breath, tried to calm down
myself, and went to the stage. I sat at the
edge of the bench, my arms relaxed and
straight in front of me. I started playing.
My fingers glided over the keys. After
a few minutes, the melody stopped. I
calmly bowed to the audience.

Lydia
Nikki Suza

Untitled

Livia Bednarz

Her black hair glittered in the light
Glazed in the sunshine
As the dark circles within her eyes held up the blockade

Every now and again they would fill up
The tears would spill, decorating her face in ornaments of
hurt

For now, though, she was beautiful
Yet so alone

With quivering hands, she would assess her fingers
Tiny, delicate
Frantically trying to scrub the red stains away
But devoid of emotion, her pale skin crumbled easily
Did she regret it?

She was beautiful now
But so alone

His smile had been an exuberant beam
Fading now with no sunshine left to illuminate it inside
She so desperately wanted to caress his face
But the aching pit of loneliness inside couldn't be quashed
He would have kissed every waterfall that spilled down
her cheeks
With a smile could have melted the stains away
He could have saved her

But she was beautiful now
Yet so alone

So very alone

Rainbow
Guy Ben-Zeev

Untitled
Marek Hertzler
Untitled
Marek Hertzler

Image 1
Taryn Liu
Harris's sparrow

**Untitl
Anonymo

The Ripple Effect
Charlie Bush

The World I revolve Around
Alejandra Arrellin

First day of school,
I walk in the room. Big T, with baggy jeans, and some 11's
on.
All eyez on me.
No spoken words, but them stares say a lot.
Pick a desk, okay now pick a partner.
Fuck. Shit. it's that one kid who got rejected by the popula
chick.

Motherfucka I'm embarrassed because now I'm definitely the
girl who likes to be reckless.

You will never know me so quit acting like you do.
A home girl can get ratchet when She wants to, you don't
decide that.
Don't mistake her for a hood rat tho
she's just like you: grew up with mental problems, has
divorced parents, has siblings she annoys, loves all kinds of
hits you like too.

Although we are alike, we also have our differences.
I know a language only a couple students speak here at school.
And even if i do, not even a few think the way I do.
My dialect, people call it ghetto, ratchet, comical, I call it
home. This is something nobody can ever snatch away from
me.
I'm confident enough to not give a damn what you call it.
I know myself, and I know when AND where to speak
White".

For God's sake it's not even about race.
Yes I might get culture shocked when I go to my White or
Asian friend's house, but thats all to that.
It's not that deep.
Some of my family members don't understand this concept.
They only know what they've been told, "hate the white folks
because they are bad people."
It makes me sad that my people are ignorant because this cruel
world only taught them the easiest and fastest way out, and
that doesnt leave room for the bigger picture.
Now my people choose to be the same because they've never
been taught that change is a good thing.
Yet again, I don't know their right from wrong.

Becoming
Anna Allport

Curiosity
Anna Allport

Ephemeral
Shannon Lin

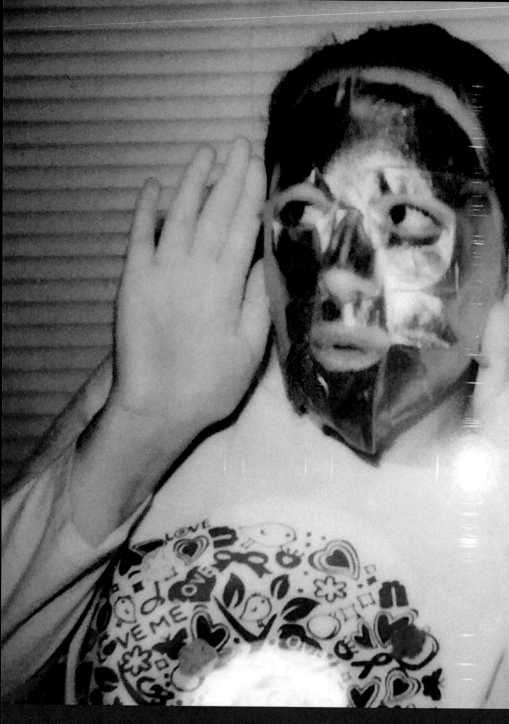

Self-portrait
Sofía Sierra-García

Wild Animal
Mishaal Hussain

Hands up, back away, slowly,
Because I am a wild animal.

And if I can't see that you are unarmed, I will bite.
And if you come too close, I will run.
Don't lose eye contact,
Without it I lose trust in your intentions.
But do not stare me down,
I will curl so tightly into myself that you won't be able to
find me again.

My body is small, fragile, and weak,
compared to yours.
You forget that your jokes can run me ragged,
And your fun can leave me shattered on the ground.

A laugh and I'll clasp my hands over my ears
and squeeze my eyes tightly shut
as if that can remove the sweet sound
So loud that it splits my bones.
A hug can leave me battered
And a conversation might as well have happened on
death's door.

It is possible to coax me out of my shell,
The one I use to cower away from you.

Be patient with me,
and I will be able to look you in the eye
without having to look past you.
I'll smile back at you
Instead of flinching when I see your teeth.
Talk with you
Without my voice sounding like it's been captured by the
breeze.
Melt into your touch
without it being a feverish shock.

But it will take time.
I promise I'll try
To meet your eyes,
To return your smile,
To speak up.

And when I can't
Be patient,
Speak a bit softer,
No sudden acts,
I'm trying,
and I know you are too.

But I am a wild animal
And every step forward runs the risk of three steps back.
Once you have my trust be careful with it,
It's a fragile thing,
And if you break it,
Even when you regain it,
It will always, always, be cracked.

Remember

Nina Newhouse

I remember a time when emotion was non-existent—
    a time where feeling numbness and apathy was
considered normal.
I remember hearing my great-aunt's passing,
    and I remained dry-eyed.
I remember hiding under the table during a science lab
    denying that I felt defeated.
I remember suppressing any incoming sadness
    with a bland joke that I dryly laughed at.
I remember denying feeling I had
    apart from happiness and excitement.
I remember always saying "good"
    when someone asked me how I was doing.
I remember having anxiety in my life
    but never telling anyone except for a paper notebook.
I remember never coming to terms with myself
    and realizing that it was okay to experience emotion.
I remember, with time, gathering courage and telling people
    how I actually felt.
I remember feeling liberated and loved,
    for normalizing emotion in my life.

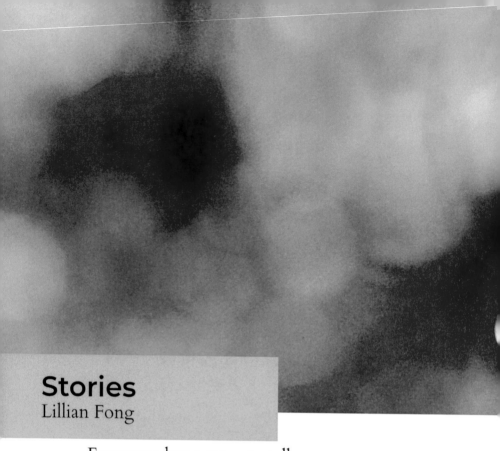

Stories
Lillian Fong

Everyone has a story to tell.

Sometimes they're of sadness, of happiness, of everything in between. But everyone's is different.

The stories that you hear—the ones on the news, the books that are published, the songs no one can stop singing—those come from the people who are the loudest. The boldest, the most willing. The ones who said, "This is something I should share with the world. This is my story, and it's worth telling."

There's a secret, and it's something people never tell you: *Everyone has a story worth telling.*

It might not seem like it at first.

No, because there are people that will knock you down and bad things that will happen and everything else that makes the world feel like it wants you to stay quiet. To stay in your good little shell, that's the way. That people like you never do anything important.

Guess what?

World in a Drop
Rina Newhouse

(It's all a lie.)

Why do you think those people, the ones who told the stories you know— why do you think they told their stories in the first place? You don't think they were scared, that they thought they would be torn to pieces, too?

Even if you think you're worthless, like nothing is anything anymore, someone will still listen. More than that, they'll want to listen. Your story could be the one that saves someone else's life.v

And some people will never be able to tell their stories. That's okay. Because it is hard, and it is scary. Sometimes it's just too much to let go of.

If you let go of the bad things, it gets easier to hold onto the good things. And once you can hold onto the good things, everything just becomes a little easier.

The world need more good things in it. And who knows, maybe you can be someone who helps make it happen.

Everyone has a story to tell—but will you tell yours? 33

Untitled
Anonymous

What is on our Minds...

C. J. Chariot

Written in reversal format: reads forwards & backwards by line.

Quantity
Is more important than
Quality
Because
Teachers will be happy with your work
What is important
Is
A variety of the number of subjects you work on
And not much of
The focused kind
Trying hard to work towards one goal
And
Thinking about your future
Can influence you into
A good lifestyle
Or
A bad lifestyle
Your motto
Will never become
"I need to do this"
So
All you need to do is what you really love.

butterfly
Rohan Bhave

Untitled
Jay Li

The City
Guy Ben-Zeev

flamingo
Rohan Bhave

Electric Stars
Jessica Wang

It's the best part of a night flight when the city lights come into view.

We angled downwards, and suddenly I had a full view of the skyline-grid, twinkling gold and white against the velvet night. It was so dark that the sky and land merged into one inky backdrop, with only the electric stars shining through. Like stars, they pulsed and shone. And as we dipped our wings downward, it was so beautiful a view.

Moments like those make it hard to believe that civilization could be anything but a wonder. It's hard to believe that every light down there might have replaced countless trees. It's hard to believe that we occupy the earth with our poisoned roots of metal.

The view was beautiful just as fireworks are dazzling even as they choke air from the sky.

Then we landed with a rush and a roar, and the airport buildings went glittering and racing by. Just as quickly as we had accelerated, the giant metal creature slowed to a graceful halt. Then I realized that my hands were clasped tightly together in front of my chest, for I had been stunned by the image of our print on the planet.

Layers
Caroline Ro 41

Exhibit
Marek Hertzl

Hide and Seek

Madeline Lurie

she is no longer
broken.

broken here. broken
with you broken by
you broken into you
like

little shards of you have permeated her heart and
she can't breathe nor bleed any longer because she
is an empty space endless groundlessness the
inside of your eyelids, a blind sense of terror good
god you say you're innocent but your words are liars
they betray you

she is not yours they sneer can't you see,
but no, you are blind insisting on seeing
and she is seeing insisting on fading.

away, away up and
away from you.

she is gone because you
are lost and she has lost
you
wandering, both hider and
seeker looking and blinded
lost and found another day,
maybe.

she is gone because you are
lost. she is gone because she
has lost you.

it's funny really you losing her when you're lost in
yourself in the labyrinths of lies and the books of
what's said, said and done

maybe someday she looks at you and
says your holy grail of words "it's all my
fault none of it was real besides, i'm
just crazy anyways"

maybe someday you find happiness in a
fast fleeting second that runs away on
quick fearful feet.

maybe someday she runs
away instead of your
happiness or rather with it.

maybe someday she loses

you lose your happiness
gains freedom. or maybe your
happiness loses its hold on you
when you lose her.

it's all the same hide and seek lost and
found going and gone up and away
another day maybe you could see things
clearly another day she leaves you see.

it's all the same to hide away while someone is
seeking to lose in the moment you find something you
never wanted to be true, that the moment she's going
is the moment she's gone and lost to you: up and
away, running away, running from running to another day.

it's all the same.

she's hiding away from you, from the memories
scared of what she'll find hide and seek to run away
another day, going, and going, and you should know by now
she is stubborn once she is going she is already gone she
was already gone months before – so to speak – the
running can be all in her head in yours, on hamster wheels
going nowhere, but quickly in other days you were not this
broken.

in other days she never felt the need to
run away up, up and away hiding away
but finding herself anyways.

Right:
Kid
Sofía Sierra-García

44

Wolf

Emily Sheng

If You Were My Friend
Anika Seshadri

If you were a genuine friend it would dawn upon you... that
we only hung out after
days of contorting my schedule and pleading,
just for you to reject my company,
with numerous moments of painful misleading.
If you were my friend
then you would have sensed my pain and let me share
a part of my story to end this frustrating spell. Instead you
locked up your paper and threw away the pens leaving my
torn pages to mend themselves.
You created new alliances
and broke ours in the process.
I learned to breathe under waves of negativity
and you didn't even notice.
You ascended the ladder
and left me on the bottom rung.
While you were having the time of your life realizing who
you'd become.
You stole my laugh from my throat
and ripped my smile from my face.
Leaving me a tattered puppet
for you to sow back into place.

If you were my friend
you would have been the light in my suffocating darkness.
Fashioning my smile when I never could.
So I'd always feel cherished
rather than isolated and misunderstood.
Now I know you were anything but my friend
and to my confidence you were a deterrent, because I've
found the true meaning of friendship
in someone who's everything you weren't.

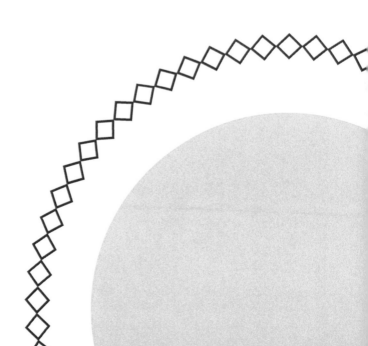

Heartstrings
Charlesy Chen

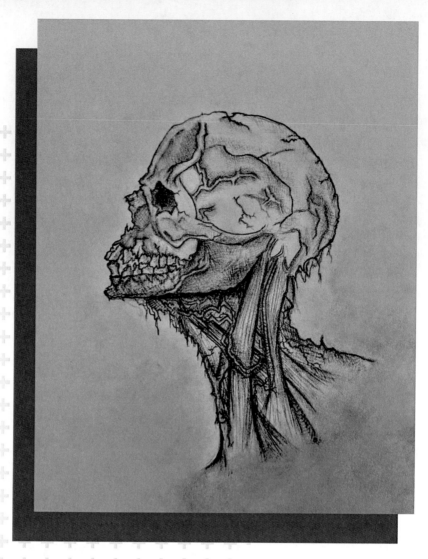

Zombie
Charlesy Chen

the paved path
Carly Feng

it's 3am, and i trudge
down the paved sidewalk
grayish hair in clouded
moonlight; above me,
streetlights every quarter
mile. and i keep my
eyes glued on my boots,
one foot after the other. but
is that all there is?
streetlights forever?

Untitled
Jessica Wang

San Diego Sea Gull
Charlie Bush

Melting
Sofía Sierra-García

Untitled
Anonymous

When I went to Vegas for the first time, the city stunned me with the large amount of neon lights and the fast-paced lifestyle. The motion blur empha-sizes the streaking taillights, purposefully showing the fast-moving lifestyle.

it's hard to make yellow not look like cheese

Sophia Lu

I am just some Latina

Inés Garcia

Written in reversal format: reads forwards & backwards by line.

I am just some Latina
And I refuse to believe that
I can follow my dreams into that beautiful blue *cielo*.
I realize this may be a shock, but
Society's stereotypes do not define you
Is a lie that we have been coarsely taught
I am destined to have no destiny
In 30 years, I will tell my children that
I have my priorities straight as
Following the status quo
Is more important than
Writing your own *destino*
I tell you this:
Once upon a time
I knew I could do or be anything, and defy the cliché story
that I was told to live
But this will not come to pass
The elites of my society tell me
I cannot expect greatness in life, or that I am fated to never
reach Their expectations,
Tantalizing as a blushing *mamey*
I do not conclude that
My dreams of giving my *café* colored brothers and sisters
their own Renaissance will come true

In the future,
We will be nothing but mere specks of dust, drifting in
America's shining, blinding light
No longer can it be said that
We can rise up, and dazzle Them with our vivacious, color-
ful culture
It will be evident that
We are forgotten, forbidden from sampling the sweet nectar
that They call the American Dream
It is foolish to presume that
We have a chance of defying Them, and their sharpened
words that pierce our skin like *lanzas*
And all of this will come true **unless we reverse it**

Only Him
Nikki Suzani

Words were chanted across the square, that he must suffer
for what he has done, that she must watch his brutal sacri-
fice and promise to never again break their dear Christian
law.

For there was no hope for him to live content. All because
of the person he loved.

Did he regret it? He should. Yet, he still remembered that
aching feeling of loneliness that left holes in his soul that
could only be filled by something he would never reach.

Until she arrived in his world. Sunshine whose rays only licked his skin but never could get close enough to warm his heart. Yet, somehow, they did.

And now he was to get burned.

Burned for sneaking kisses behind the barn. A first move that landed him in the deepest of the water but when those lips felt so right around his own he could not bear to take it back.

Burned for that soft-feeling delight when he knelt her face towards his and let them both take what they had longed for the entire day.

Burned for feeling joy as he caressed her face, holding her tears with his shoulders and lifting her up so that she could see the world in new directions. Holding her in his arms and kissing every waterfall that spilled down her face until she could find her own beauty within.

Burned for longing to be a true couple, longing to meet her parents and whisk her away into the countryside where they would dance among the olive trees until the very dawn.

Burned for being too poor for her, too dumb for her, and worst of all… Too black for her.

And negroes who loved whitefolk deserved to burn in hell.

pawn shop

Liza Kolbasov

we stare into the windows of 24/7 CVS stores, into puddles crawling down streets, into screens reflecting the edges of someone else's world, into anything but the messes of our own hearts. fiddle with pens, with the laces on our shoes, with the knobs on our wrist watches. live in the sound of feet tap-tapping across the street—towards us— then away.

yesterday, I found a glove left behind on a street corner— between 31st and main. drowning out my thoughts with another's voice, I almost ignored it. it is worn, and has no pair. its owner will probably buy another tomorrow. falling in and out of lives, leaving no mark— how many people pass me by? who left me on the corner of 31st and main?

I see someone's eyes staring at me from the window of the corner CVS. she meets me there daily and never says hello. strange how we're taught never to talk to ourselves. I listen to the tap of feet on the street and fiddle with the knobs of the wrist watch someone else used to own and probably never loved. I look away.

reaching into my pocket, I pull out a single gray glove. on the way home, I listen for footsteps, but, as usual, they only fade away. I almost smile at the girl in the CVS window, but think better of it. I turn the corner of 31st and main without looking down. alone in a photocopy life, listening as footsteps tap away. I walk into the pawnshop, considering buying a new pair of gloves, and decide that I am going to sell my wristwatch.

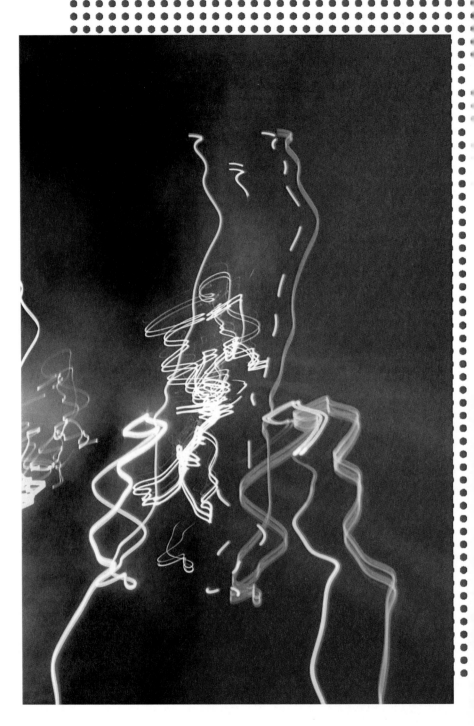

Tremors
Justin Chiao